ThemeWorks™
An Integrated Curriculum for Young Children

Rain

Joan Westley
Illustrated by Elaine Abe

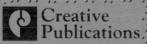
Creative Publications

THEMEWORKS™: RAIN

Creative Publications is a registered trademark.

With special thanks to Betsy Verne Franco and Holly Melton.

Grateful acknowledgement is made to the teachers and children who tried these materials in their classrooms:

Marlene Getz ◆ Berkeley, California
Kathleen Hammer ◆ Mountain View, California
Becky Kenfield ◆ Missoula, Montana
Kathy Muench ◆ Schaumberg, Illinois
Carolyn Nuite ◆ San Francisco, California
Claire Piccinelli ◆ Redway, California
Pearl Seidman ◆ Concord, California

Grateful acknowledgement is also made to Penguin Books USA Inc. for permission to reprint their copyrighted material listed below.

From UMBRELLA by Taro Yashima. Copyright ©1953 by Taro Yashima, renewed 1986 by Taro Yashima. Used by permission of Viking Penguin, a division of Penguin Books USA Inc.

From BRINGING THE RAIN TO KAPITI PLAIN by Verna Aardema, illustrated by Beatriz Vidal. Text copyright ©1981 by Verna Aardema. Illustrations copyright ©1981 by Beatriz Vidal. Used by permission of Dial Books for Young Readers, a division of Penguin Books USA Inc.

Project Manager: Micaelia Randolph Brummett

Research Editor: Ann Roper
Graphic Designer: JoAnne Hammer
Production Artists: Normajean Franco and Roy Kutsunai

©1991 Creative Publications
1300 Villa Street
Mountain View, CA 94041
Printed U.S.A.
ISBN: 1-56107-077-7

5 6 7 8 9 10. 9 6 5 4

Table of Contents

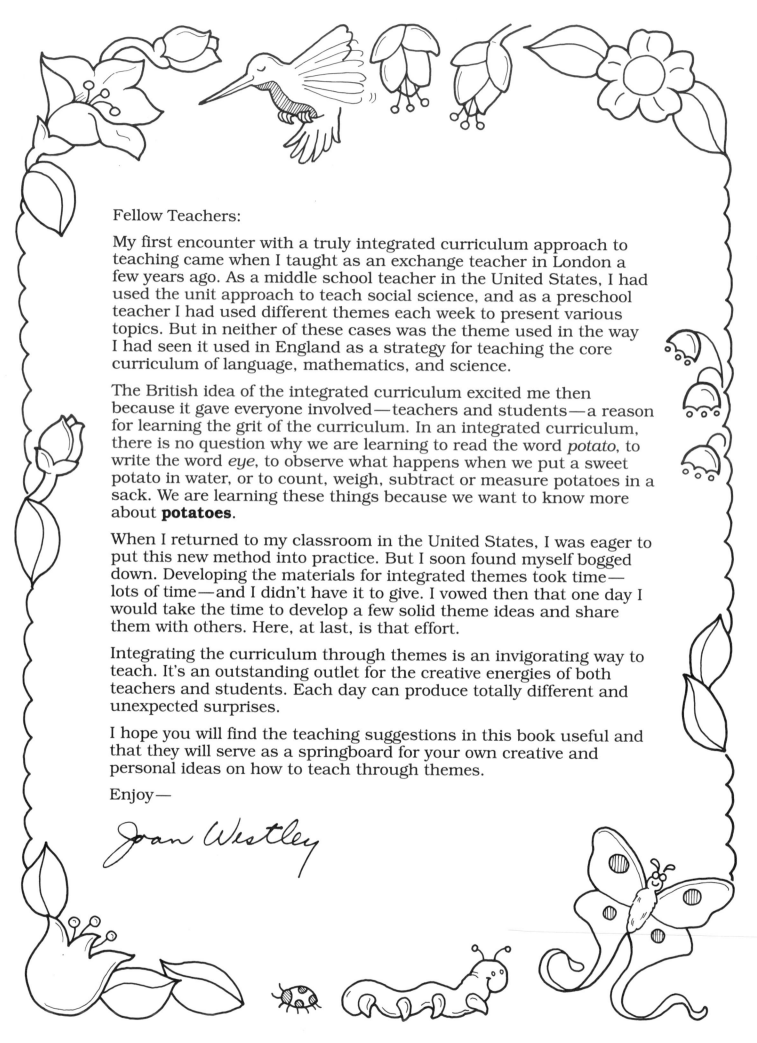

Fellow Teachers:

My first encounter with a truly integrated curriculum approach to teaching came when I taught as an exchange teacher in London a few years ago. As a middle school teacher in the United States, I had used the unit approach to teach social science, and as a preschool teacher I had used different themes each week to present various topics. But in neither of these cases was the theme used in the way I had seen it used in England as a strategy for teaching the core curriculum of language, mathematics, and science.

The British idea of the integrated curriculum excited me then because it gave everyone involved—teachers and students—a reason for learning the grit of the curriculum. In an integrated curriculum, there is no question why we are learning to read the word *potato*, to write the word *eye*, to observe what happens when we put a sweet potato in water, or to count, weigh, subtract or measure potatoes in a sack. We are learning these things because we want to know more about **potatoes**.

When I returned to my classroom in the United States, I was eager to put this new method into practice. But I soon found myself bogged down. Developing the materials for integrated themes took time— lots of time—and I didn't have it to give. I vowed then that one day I would take the time to develop a few solid theme ideas and share them with others. Here, at last, is that effort.

Integrating the curriculum through themes is an invigorating way to teach. It's an outstanding outlet for the creative energies of both teachers and students. Each day can produce totally different and unexpected surprises.

I hope you will find the teaching suggestions in this book useful and that they will serve as a springboard for your own creative and personal ideas on how to teach through themes.

Enjoy—

Joan Westley

Teaching Notes

What is *ThemeWorks*™ ?

ThemeWorks is a series of teacher resource books created especially for prekindergarten through grade two teachers who wish to use an integrated approach to teaching the curriculum. Each *ThemeWorks* book centers on one powerful theme. As the children investigate the theme, they engage naturally in language, math, science, cooking, poetry, literature, dramatization and art activities. The theme also provides a springboard for large-scale projects, dramatic play centers, and the construction of classroom environments.

ThemeWorks heavily favors the whole language approach to developing language skills. Children are exposed to language through chants, songs, stories, poems, and rhymes. They are encouraged to play with the rhythmic and repetitive structures in rhymes and chants and they begin the process of writing using these frames. Reading is developed through the children's own speaking and writing.

Counting and number work are developed through meaningful problems that evolve out of real situations relevant to the theme. Emphasis is on number concepts and relationships, organizing numerical data, and measurement.

How were the themes chosen?

There are hundreds of possibilities for themes, but the best themes are those that provide the potential for a broad range of activities across all the curriculum areas. We chose themes that were rich sources for songs, poems, storybooks, and rhymes. Also considered was the theme's appropriateness for the developmental levels and interests of young children. The themes addressed in this first series of 64-page books are:

    Night Time
    Rain
    Houses
    Trees
    At the Seashore
    Under the Ground

How is *ThemeWorks*™ organized?

Each theme is organized into three distinct parts:

- the kickoff,
- the theme activities, and
- the culminating event.

We recommend that each class do the kickoff and the culminating event and then pick the activities they would prefer to do in between. This arrangement allows an individual class to make a theme study as personal as possible and to adjust the length of time devoted to a particular theme to meet individual needs.

What is the kickoff?

We begin each theme with a kickoff event related to the theme. For example, the exploration of the night time theme kicks off with a pretend sleepover at school. This activity gives everyone involved a sense of expectation about the theme that is to be studied.

The kickoff is designed to capitalize on what children already know about the topic rather than require any specialized knowledge or skills. It also provides an informal assessment of what students already know about a topic. It starts them focusing their thinking on what they want to learn about the theme.

The theme mascot is also introduced during the kickoff. This mascot is a puppet character that serves to give instructions, introduce new ideas and songs, and provide friendly guidance throughout the theme study.

This is also a good time to begin a theme web and a word bank.

What is a web?

A web is a brainstorming tool and graphic organizer. At the center of the web is the name of the current theme. As children name subtopics of the theme, each idea is connected to the center by lines. Through this brainstorming process, the class begins to see all the avenues of exploration that are available to them through the vehicle of the theme. Work on the web can go on throughout the investigation of the theme. A sample web is shown on page 8.

What is a word bank?

A word bank is a dictionary of words related to the theme. Entries for the word bank may be suggested by the children any time throughout the exploration of the theme. A sample word bank is shown on page 8.

What happens after the kickoff?

Between the opening and culminating events, each *ThemeWorks* resource book offers 18 mini-topics related to the theme at large. Each mini-topic is presented on a two-page spread. By scanning the Table of Contents, a teacher can choose those topics she feels are most appropriate for her class's study of the theme at hand.

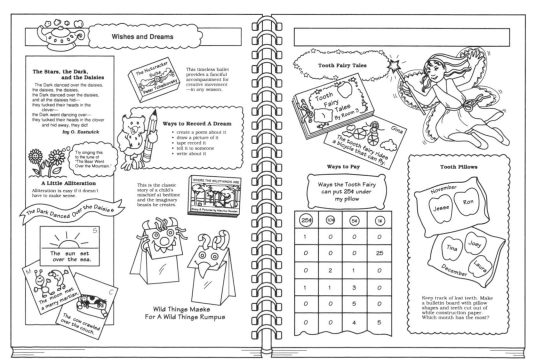

How does the theme exploration end?

At the end of each *ThemeWorks* book is a suggestion for a culminating event. In Night Time, for example, the theme study culminates in a pretend campout at school. Each of the events is an outgrowth of many of the theme activities that have gone before. Throughout the theme exploration, children prepare for the culminating event by creating special artwork or construction projects that form the environment of the final event. The culminating event is a good way to end the theme exploration because it gives students a sense of accomplishment, and a chance to show what they know. The children present some of the work they have done, sing the songs they have learned, play some of the games—all within a context relevant to the theme.

The Rain

The Rain theme is best explored when you are likely to have some actual rain to see and hear, touch and smell. In much of the country, spring is the most appropriate time for studying rain because the effects of rain are apparent everywhere—swollen river banks, rain puddles, bursts of color from blossoming bulbs.

We launch our theme with a favorite early childhood topic—the clothes we wear—and end with a walk over the rainbow. Through the rain theme, we explore clouds, predict when rain will fall, go for a walk in the rain, build Noah's ark, measure rain, explore puddles, make desert and jungle environments, have a rain dance, and take a journey to the jungle.

A Rain Web

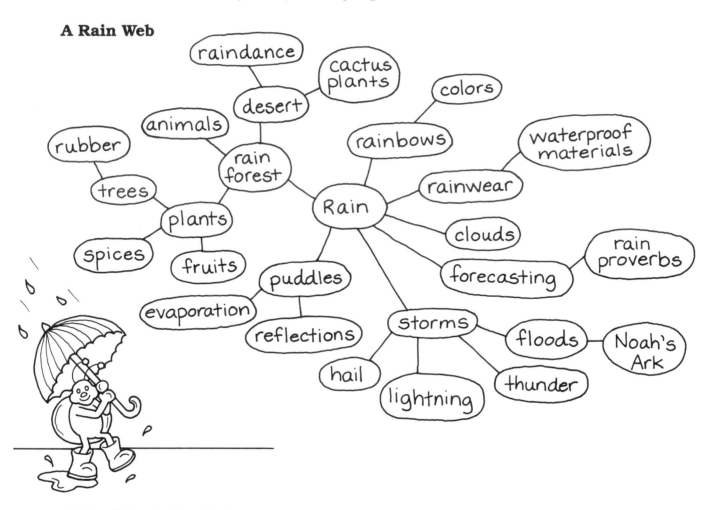

A Word Bank for Rain

rain	duck	thunder	puddle	parrot
boot	sun	lightning	desert	fern
umbrella	cloud	water	jungle	banana
raincoat	raindrop	mushroom	rain forest	rubber
rain hat	shower	wet	cactus	rain dance
poncho	flower	dry	camel	rainbow

THEMEWORKS™ : Rain
©1991 Creative Publications

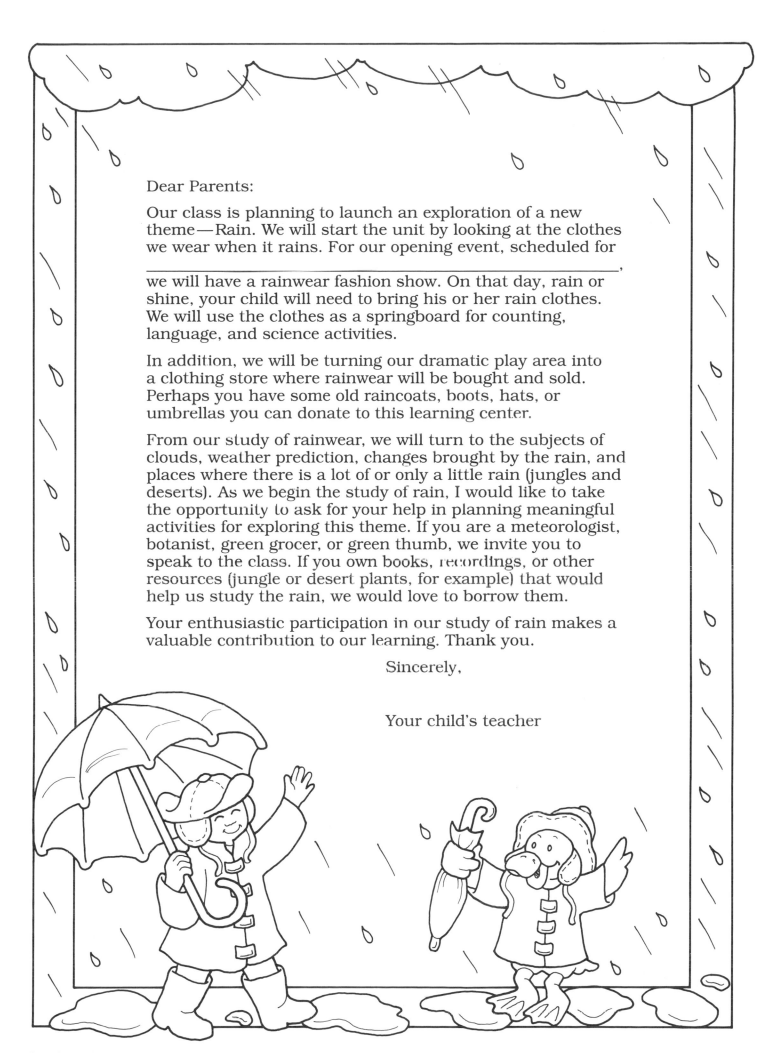

Dear Parents:

Our class is planning to launch an exploration of a new theme—Rain. We will start the unit by looking at the clothes we wear when it rains. For our opening event, scheduled for

_____,

we will have a rainwear fashion show. On that day, rain or shine, your child will need to bring his or her rain clothes. We will use the clothes as a springboard for counting, language, and science activities.

In addition, we will be turning our dramatic play area into a clothing store where rainwear will be bought and sold. Perhaps you have some old raincoats, boots, hats, or umbrellas you can donate to this learning center.

From our study of rainwear, we will turn to the subjects of clouds, weather prediction, changes brought by the rain, and places where there is a lot of or only a little rain (jungles and deserts). As we begin the study of rain, I would like to take the opportunity to ask for your help in planning meaningful activities for exploring this theme. If you are a meteorologist, botanist, green grocer, or green thumb, we invite you to speak to the class. If you own books, recordings, or other resources (jungle or desert plants, for example) that would help us study the rain, we would love to borrow them.

Your enthusiastic participation in our study of rain makes a valuable contribution to our learning. Thank you.

Sincerely,

Your child's teacher

A Rainwear Fashion Show

The Parade

Our opening event is a rainwear fashion show. It can be held any day, rain or shine. The children bring to school all of their rain gear—boots, raincoats, ponchos, umbrellas, rain hats. (See Parent Letter on page 9.) Then they parade around the room wearing their rain gear. The teacher announces each child and describes what the child is wearing—to a round of applause.

Just Like You

The children parade around the room until they hear a clap of thunder (a drum beat). Then they find someone who is wearing rain gear that is like their own rain gear in some way (color, same kind of buckles, and so on). They must be able to tell how they are alike.

Happiness

John had
Great Big
Waterproof
Boots on;
John had a
Great Big
Waterproof
Hat;
John had a
Great Big
Waterproof
Macintosh—
And that
Said John
Is
That.

A. A. Milne

Children can chant this poem over and over either orally or reading from a pocket chart. Substituting their names and what they are wearing adds variety and motivation to the readings.

What Are You Wearing?

(a parody of *Mary Wears a Red Dress All Day Long*)

C
Mary wears red boots,

G7   C
Red boots, red boots.

C
Mary wears red boots

G7   C
When it rains.

This song can be modified easily to describe anyone in the class. For example:

Carlos wears a yellow slicker,
Yellow slicker, a yellow slicker.
Carlos wears a yellow slicker
When it rains.

THEMEWORKS™ : Rain
©1991 Creative Publications

Guess My Secret Rule

The teacher names children whose rain clothing fits and does not fit the secret rule. The secret rule might be *coats with zippers*, *boots with buckles*, *yellow hats*, and so on. Those children the teacher names who are wearing clothing that fits the secret rule are sent to one side of the classroom. Those who are not wearing clothes that fit the secret rule are sent to the other side of the room. Everyone tries to figure out what the secret rule is.

Rainwear Word Bank

boots	rain hat
umbrella	slicker
raincoat	poncho

Introducing Edward the Duck

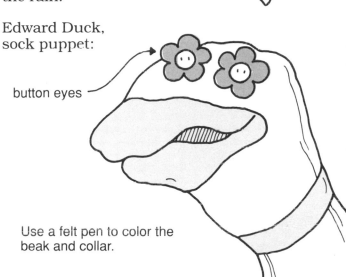

Edward Duck, our mascot for this theme, will sing to us, tell us stories, and explain things we don't understand. Like most ducks, Edward likes water, and doesn't mind getting wet in the rain.

Edward Duck, sock puppet:

button eyes

Use a felt pen to color the beak and collar.

Boot Patterns

Boot shapes are on page 52.

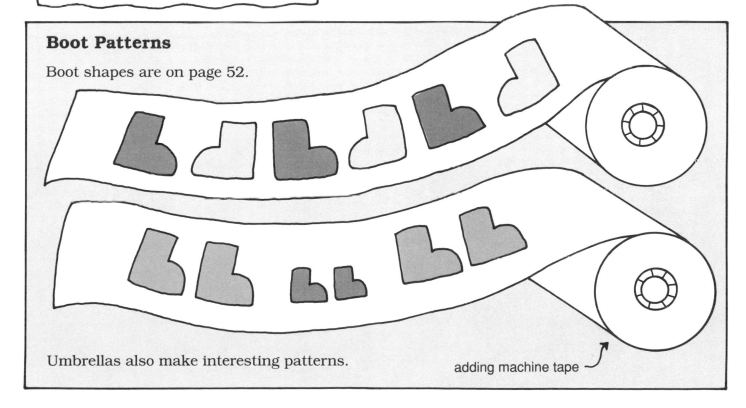

adding machine tape

Umbrellas also make interesting patterns.

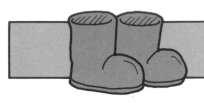

Rainy Day Clothes

Dramatic Play: Clothing Store

In their dramatic play, children will naturally make size comparisons, measure feet for boots, talk about attributes such as color and design, and use play money to mimic buying merchandise. In setting up the clothing store, they may classify the merchandise by type or color, or arrange the merchandise by size. They might also make up price tags for the rain gear for sale.

Clothing (merchandise)
   boots
   raincoats
   umbrellas
   rain hats
   ponchos

Props
   clothing racks
   hangers
   ruler or
     measuring stick
   cash register
   play money
   price tags

Roles
   clerks
   customers

Clothing Store Inventory

RAINDROP OUTLET	
boots	Ⳋ
umbrellas	Ⳋ I
raincoats	III
ponchos	IIII

25¢

50¢

Class Visitor

A shoe salesperson could be invited to speak to the class about different kinds of rain boots and how feet are measured for fitting.

On the Bookshelf

When Momo receives an umbrella for her birthday, she can hardly wait for rain to fall.

THEMEWORKS™ : Rain
©1991 Creative Publications

Absorbency Experiments

The children put drops of water on different kinds of materials (vinyl, terry cloth, oil cloth, waxed paper, tissue paper, rubber, aluminum foil, plastic, cotton, wool, nylon, and so on) to see whether they absorb or repel water.

On the Bookshelf

This book explains why ducks don't get wet in the rain and other interesting facts about ducks.

Clothing Designers

Project: Designing a rain outfit for a paper doll (see page 53).

The children can use what they found out in the absorbency experiments to choose materials that are waterproof. They can cut out material to fit the doll and then paste the cutout clothes on the doll.

Rainy Day

I do not like a rainy day.
The road is wet, the sky is gray.
They dress me up, from head to toes.
In lots and lots of rubber clothes.
I wish the sun would come and stay.
I do not like a rainy day.

William Wise

Will It Rain?

Rain Proverbs

Ring around the moon.
Rain is coming soon.

If chickens roll in sand,
Rain is sure to be at hand.

Red sky at night,
Sailor's delight.
Red sky in the morning,
Sailors take warning.

Rain before seven,
Shine before eleven.

A sunshiny shower
Won't last an hour.

Our Own Proverbs

It will rain, Amy
If you see a goat get on a train.

It will rain, Wes
If you see a horse with a white mane.

It will rain, Sara
If you see a mouse on a weather vane.

On the Bookshelf

A January Fog Will Freeze a Hog and other weather folklore
Hubert Davis ill. by John Wallner

A compilation of weather folklore.

Rain Rhymes

train	Dane	vain
lane	gain	vane
Spain	grain	pane
pain	stain	plane
crane	plain	
cane		
main		
mane		
drain		

Weather Forecasting

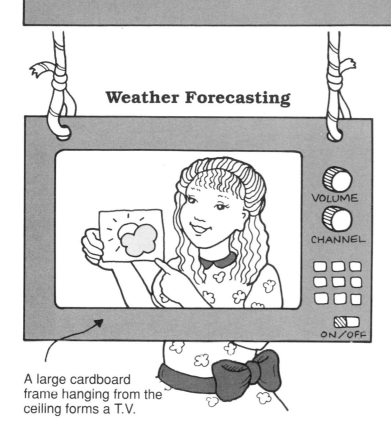

A large cardboard frame hanging from the ceiling forms a T.V.

Each morning, a different child can take the role of the weather forecaster and predict the day's weather.

Meet a Meteorologist

A class visit to a television station could be arranged. Or, a meteorologist could be invited to speak to the class.

Signs of Rain

dark sky
black clouds
getting colder
loud wind
lightning & thunder
leaves blowing

Will It Rain Today?

children's self-portraits

_____ think it will rain.

_____ think it will not rain.

Cloud Watching

Watch the Clouds

On a cloudy day, we lie down in the playground or a field, faces to the sky but looking away from the sun. We talk about what we see. Observations are recorded in an experience chart.

Clouds

fluffy
soft
white
like whipped cream
like cauliflower
slow moving
thick
bright
puffy

Questions:

- Look at one cloud. What can you tell about it? What color is it? What size?

- What shape is your cloud? What does it remind you of?

- Is your cloud moving? How can you tell? Is it moving fast or slow? Which way is it moving? Are all the clouds moving the same way?

- What happens when the sun goes behind a cloud?

Cloud Timeline

9:00   10:00   11:00   12:00   1:00

Polaroid® pictures taken from the classroom window.

THEMEWORKS™ : Rain
©1991 Creative Publications

Parachute Cloud

The children make a cloud by holding the edge of a parachute and moving it to mimic the activity of a cloud. After they have freely explored the parachute for a while, direct their movement with a fantasy like this:

A Rain Cloud floated above the sea, moving slowly toward the land. When it got to the land, the winds started to blow it around. It blew this way and that way. It moved faster and faster. Then the wind stopped. The rain cloud kept moving but more slowly now. When it came to a mountain it had to climb up and up to get over the mountain. As it climbed it got bigger and bigger and heavier and heavier. Finally, it could no longer hold the water droplets in it, and it rained.

Cloud Collage

Cloud Materials:
    cotton balls
    white tissue paper
    white tissues
    packing material
    white fabric

On the Bookshelf

An anthropomorphic cloud tries not to rain and disturb the people below, until it spots a farmer who welcomes the rain.

On the Bookshelf

It Looked Like Spilt Milk
by Charles G Shaw

In this classic storybook, we see clouds that look like rabbits, birds, and ice cream cones.

I Like Clouds

I like clouds.

Fluffy clouds.

Puffy clouds.

White clouds.

Bright clouds.

Any kind of cloud.

I like clouds.

Cloud Mobile

The clouds on this mobile are made by cutting out a cloud shape from two sheets of white construction paper. The two shapes are then stapled together and stuffed with newspaper.

The children can cut out cloud shapes that remind them of other things (like spilt milk). Then when the clouds are finished and displayed as a mobile, children can take turns describing their clouds (*My cloud looks like ____*) with the others guessing which cloud is being described.

THEMEWORKS™ : Rain
©1991 Creative Publications

Cloud Pudding

4 cups frozen blueberries
6 egg whites
1 pint whipping cream
½ cup sugar
juice of 1 lemon

Mix sugar and lemon. Add fruit.
Beat egg whites and fold in. Whip
the cream and fold in.

Children are amazed at the
transformation when cream
and egg whites are whipped.

Cloudburst

Cloudburst!

This outdoor game
can be played with
the whole class,
with some of the
children (at least
five) acting as
water droplets.
The water droplets
form a cloud and
move together.

When they yell, *Cloudburst!*, they
scatter and try to catch (touch) the
other children before they can find
shelter from the rain. Anyone under
a shelter of some sort cannot be
caught by the rain. Caught players
become new water droplets for the
next round.

Hello, Black Cloud

(a parody of *Baa, Baa, Black Sheep*)

```
C                F         C
Hello, black cloud, have you any rain?

G7      C    G7           C
Yes sir, yes sir, drops and drops of rain.

C           F      C        G7
Rain for the flowers, rain for the farms,

    Dm        Am        Dm  G7   C
And rain for the little boy who lives in the lane.

C                 F          C
Hello, black cloud, have you any rain?

G7      C    G7               C
Yes sir, yes sir, drops and drops of rain.
```

One group of children sings the question
and another group answers it.

Cloudy With a Chance of Rain

Classifying Clouds

The three main cloud types:

Cirrus — feathery, high, thin

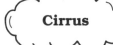

Cumulus — fluffy, thick

Stratus — low, cover the whole sky

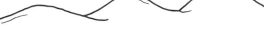

??????????????????????????????

Question Box

What is a cloud made of? The air is filled with tiny invisible water droplets called water vapor. When warm air rises to meet colder air, the water vapor condenses: it changes from a gas (water vapor) to a liquid, and becomes visible as clouds.

Children can see a cloud develop in the classroom. Heat water in a tea kettle over a hot plate. When it boils, water vapor escaping from the kettle forms a steam "cloud" as it leaves the kettle.

On the Bookshelf

THEMEWORKS™ : Rain
©1991 Creative Publications

Cloud Paint

1 cup warm water
1½ cup soap flakes

Whip with an egg beater until stiff. Then use like fingerpaint. Blue paper for sky sets off the white clouds.

Raindrops in a Cloud

Ziplock bags or small doll pillow cases work well for clouds in this activity. Start by showing the children the "cloud" and asking them to write down how many "raindrops" (gumdrops, candy kisses, interlocking cubes) they think will fit in it. Then have them fill the cloud and tell how many fit. Which guess was closest?

Our Guesses

25	100	30
	19	53
150	45	

On the Bookshelf

This adaptation of an African folk tale has a cumulative refrain like "The House that Jack Built." In the tale, Ki-pat shoots an arrow into a cloud to make the rain fall on a drought-stricken plain.

BRINGING THE RAIN TO KAPITI PLAIN by Verna Aardema / pic. by Beatriz Vidal

The cloud princess is crying.

Children might enjoy creating their own tales about how clouds and rain form.

Rainy Day Diary

10:00 — A sprinkle of raindrops is falling.

10:30 — The wind is blowing. The rain is slanted.

11:00 — We see lightning. We hear thunder. Big drops of rain are falling.

11:30 — The rain is pouring down in sheets.

It's Raining, It's Pouring

D A   D A
It's raining, it's pouring.

A   D A
The old man is snoring.

E
He bumped his head

E
When he went to bed

A
And he couldn't get up

D   A
In the morning.

Rain Word Bank

rain	mist
showers	cloudburst
sprinkle	hail
rainstorm	driving rain
thunder	pouring rain
lightning	flood
downpour	raining cats and dogs
drizzle	coming down in buckets

As new words come up in discussion, they can be added to the list.

Rain at the Water Table

Let children use a variety of objects such as sieves, colanders, misters, spray bottles, atomizers, sprinklers, and so on to mimic rain of different kinds.

Rain Frolics

One child can be the wind, another can be lightning, a few can be clouds, and the rest are raindrops. As the teacher describes different kinds of rain using words from the Rain Word Bank, they pantomime their roles in that kind of rain. If the wind blows from one direction, the raindrops should move in the other direction.

How Much Longer?

How long do you think the rain will last?   until lunch   until after school   until dinner   until bedtime   until morning

Rain on the Green Grass

Rain on the [green grass]

Rain on the [tree]

Rain on the [house top]

But not on me.

mountains

sea

forests

bee

robin

kitty cat

Rain in a Bottle

Children can watch rain form in a terrarium.

On the Bookshelf

Rain is described in all its variations from raindrops on a window pane to streams of rain flowing into the sea. Good source for the language of rain.

Rain Rain Rivers
Words & Pic. by URI SHULEVITZ

THEMEWORKS™ : Rain
©1991 Creative Publications

Rain

The rain is raining all around,
It falls on field and tree,
It rains on the umbrellas here
And on the ships at sea.

Robert Louis Stevenson

Catch the Rain

The children can set out various large containers before a rain begins and retrieve them after the storm. They can then pour the water into a tall narrow glass jar (estimating how high the water level will be first) and mark the outside of the jar to show how much rain fell in the container during the storm. Then the same container could be used in a different rainstorm to see if more or less water is collected.

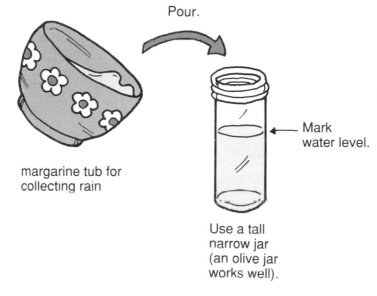

Pour.

margarine tub for collecting rain

Mark water level.

Use a tall narrow jar (an olive jar works well).

Silly Sayings

Kristin — It's raining cats and dogs.

Brandon — It's raining doors and windows.

Akiko — It's raining strawberries and ice cream.

Make drawings of cats and dogs and other nonsense.

A Walk in the Rain

Getting Ready

How better to study rain than to go out for a walk in the rain? All the senses are activated as we explore rain and its effects on the things around us. We need go no farther than the playground to get rich sources for our observations.

The best time to take a walk in the rain is when the weather is fairly warm and a light rain is falling. The children will need to be adequately dressed in waterproof clothing so that they can enjoy the experience without risk to their health. The children will also need a change of clothes so that they will have something dry to wear after the walk.

Look for It

- Find a place where the ground is dry. Figure out why it is dry there.

- Find an animal (bird, insect, or worm, for example). Is the animal in or out of the rain?

Worms come out of their holes during a rain to avoid being flooded out.

Shutterbugging

A camera with low light film provides a handy way of recording experiences on the field trip. Later, back in the classroom, children can write or dictate captions for the photographs.

We saw raindrops on pine needles.

Raindrops made rings in the puddles.

Flowers were drooping.

THEMEWORKS™ : Rain
©1991 Creative Publications

Rain Spout Explorations

- Put a can or pail under a water spout. How much rain water can you collect in one minute?

- Follow the water in a rain spout. Where does it come from? Where does it go?

On the Bookshelf

Peter Spier's RAIN

A walk in the rain — Ursel Scheffler/Ulises Wensell

A House of Leaves by Kiyoshi Soya illus. by Akiko Hayashi

A Wet and Sandy Day by Joanne Ryder — Pictures by Donald Carrick

Where does the butterfly go when it rains By May Garelick with pictures by Leonard Weisgard

Lost in the Storm by CAROL CARRICK pic. by DONALD CARRICK

THE STORM BOOK by Charlotte Zolotow pic. by Margaret Bloy Graham

Eeency Weency Spider

```
G                           D7          G
The eency weency spider went up the water spout.

G                    D7             G
Down came the rain and washed the spider out.

G                    D7          G
Out came the sun and dried up all the rain,

D7   G                      D7        G
And the eency weency spider went up the spout again.
```

Some fun variations can be created by the class. For example:

The eency weency caterpillar crawled up the maple tree.

The eency weency ladybug climbed up the yellow rose.

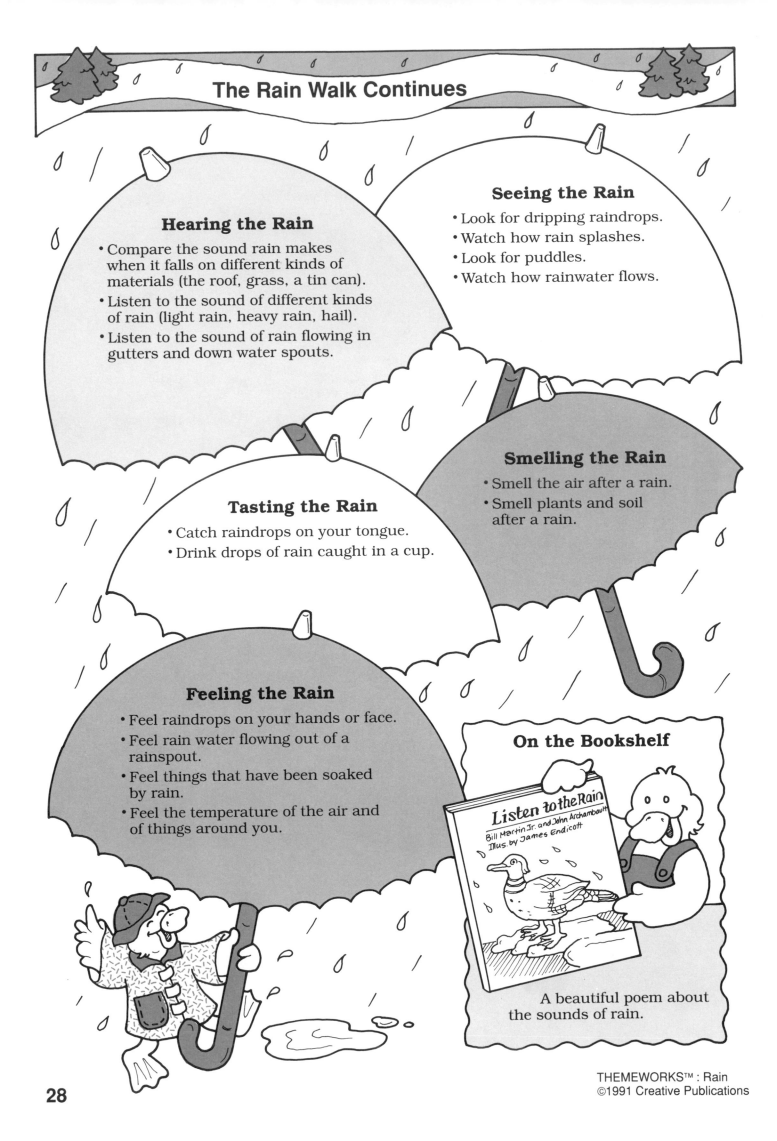

The Rain Walk Continues

Hearing the Rain

• Compare the sound rain makes when it falls on different kinds of materials (the roof, grass, a tin can).
• Listen to the sound of different kinds of rain (light rain, heavy rain, hail).
• Listen to the sound of rain flowing in gutters and down water spouts.

Seeing the Rain

• Look for dripping raindrops.
• Watch how rain splashes.
• Look for puddles.
• Watch how rainwater flows.

Tasting the Rain

• Catch raindrops on your tongue.
• Drink drops of rain caught in a cup.

Smelling the Rain

• Smell the air after a rain.
• Smell plants and soil after a rain.

Feeling the Rain

• Feel raindrops on your hands or face.
• Feel rain water flowing out of a rainspout.
• Feel things that have been soaked by rain.
• Feel the temperature of the air and of things around you.

On the Bookshelf

Listen to the Rain
Bill Martin Jr. and John Archambault
Illus. by James Endicott

A beautiful poem about the sounds of rain.

28

THEMEWORKS™ : Rain
©1991 Creative Publications

Five Senses Word Chart

See 👁	Hear 👂	Feel ☞	Smell 〰	Taste 👅
puddles raindrops mud streams splashes waterfalls	bum-bum- bum pitter-patter whooshing gurgling dripping swish-swish	wet squishy cold tickling	like dirt like grass	salty like water

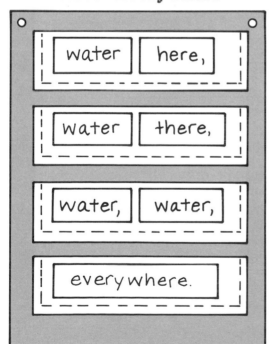

Drum Beats

Children can beat drums or play other percussion instruments to match pictures of light, heavy, windy rain, or hail. Other children can be raindrops and dance to the rain.

Water Everywhere

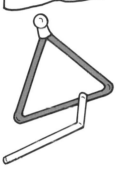
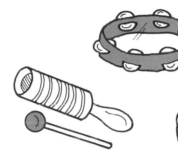

water	here,
water	there,
water,	water,
everywhere.	

For water, substitute: clouds, raindrops, umbrellas, puddles, and other things the class saw on the walk in the rain.

A-B-C Soup

6 cups water
1 qt. stewed tomatoes
1 small onion
2 carrots
2 stalks celery
other vegetables as desired
2 bay leaves
1 tsp. basil
salt and pepper to taste
½ cup alphabet noodles

Simmer tomatoes, spices, and water. Peel and chop the onion. Scrub and chop the vegetables. Add to the pot and simmer 20 minutes. Add the noodles and cook 15 minutes longer.

A cup of hot soup after a wet walk in the rain will be welcomed by everyone.

Noah's Ark

Many excellent picture books are available to help you retell this traditional story.

How are the stories alike and different?

Which is the favorite? (Make a graph to find out.)

Clay Beasts

Each child makes a pair of animals with clay. Someone should also be selected to make Noah and his family. Then all the clay beasts and Noah's family can be used in a re-enactment of the story.

Build a Boat

The children could work in small groups to make a boat (Noah's Ark) that will float and that will hold all the clay beasts. Different kinds of materials can be made available: clay or plasticene, wood scraps, aluminum foil, cardboard, Styrofoam™, margarine tubs. You'll also need a water table or plastic tub for children to use in testing whether their boats can float.

THEMEWORKS™ : Rain
©1991 Creative Publications

Songbook

The animals file into Noah's Ark one by one, then two by two, three by three, and so on to ten by ten. The music for the old folk song is given at the end of the book.

Parade of the Animals

After reading and singing *One Wide River to Cross*, the children can set up their clay beasts (or animal crackers set in playdough) in rows of one, then two, then three, then four and so on. Each time, the animals can be counted by ones, twos, threes, fours, and so on.

Ark Shapes

Counting the Animals

Rainy Day Blues

Weather Wheel

paper plate

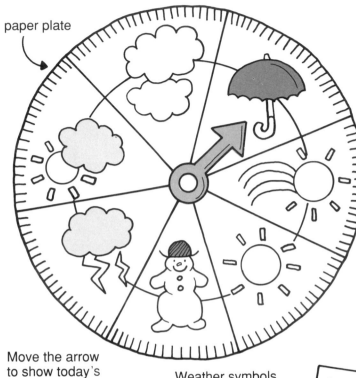

Move the arrow to show today's weather.

Weather symbols are on page 54.

Cans and Can'ts

When it rains,

I can't | ride my bike.

I can't | play outside.

But I can | read a book

jump ro... | build with blocks | play in the park | play dress-up

draw with crayons

Rain, Rain Rhymes

C
Rain, rain, go away.

C
Come again another day.

G7
Rain, rain, go away.

C   Am   G7   C
Little Johnny wants to play.

Rain, rain, go to Spain.

Never show your face again.

Calendar Count

APRIL

☂ _____7_____ days

☺ _____10_____ days

Outside/Inside Peek-a-Book

A large sheet of construction paper folded in half.

outside view

inside view

Be a Bee

Inactivity makes rainy days all the more dreary. Here are some physical movement activities just right for the rainy day blues.

- Be a worm and wiggle in the rain.
- Be a duck and waddle in the rain.
- Be a frog and jump in the rain.
- Be a rabbit and hop in the rain.
- Be a crane and stand on one foot in the rain.
- Be a spider and crawl in the rain.
- Be a snail and slither in the rain.
- Be a bee and buzz in the rain.

Peanut Butter Fudge

For groups of four:

1. Mix in a bowl:
   ½ cup peanut butter   ½ cup raisins
   1 tablespoon dry milk   1 tablespoon honey

2. Form into balls.

3. Roll in toppings: coconut, chopped nuts

Prelutsky's poem *Fudge!* in his book **Rainy Day Saturday** is a good poem to read while the children eat their peanut butter fudge.

On the Bookshelf

Grandpa tells a fanciful tale about an extraordinary rain.

Fourteen humorous poems about the pleasures and pains of a rainy day.

Raindrops

How brave a ladybug must be!
Each drop of rain is big as she.

Can you imagine what you'd do
If raindrops fell as big as you?

Aileen Fisher

Observing Raindrops

The children can shake wet hands on leaves over waxed paper, and observe the raindrops with magnifying glasses.

Some questions to explore:
- Are all the raindrops the same size and shape?
- Can you see through a raindrop?
- Can you see reflections in a raindrop?
- How do the raindrops move? Can you make a raindrop wiggle? Does the shape of the raindrop change when it moves?
- What happens when two raindrops collide?
- Can you find a way to make one big raindrop?

Raindrop Paths

Drops of colored water are blown in different directions to create artistic effects.

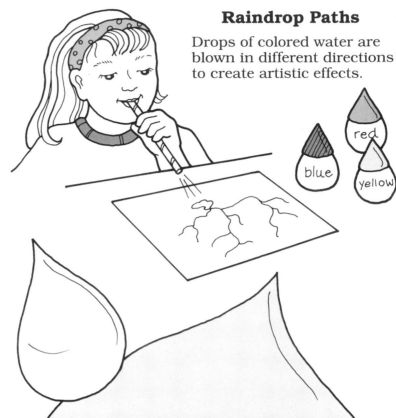

Ten Little Raindrops

F
One little, two little, three little raindrops

C7
Four little, five little, six little raindrops

F
Seven little, eight little, nine little raindrops

C7   F
Ten little raindrops fell.

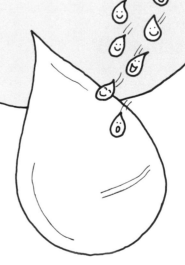

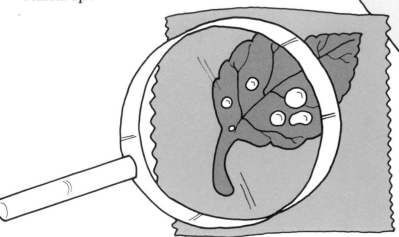

THEMEWORKS™ : Rain
©1991 Creative Publications

Showers

Squelch and squirt and squiggle,
Drizzle and drip and drain—
Such a lot of water
Comes down with the rain!

Marchette Chute

On the Bookshelf

This book follows raindrops from a puddle to the sea. Another great source for language development.

Rain Alliteration Games

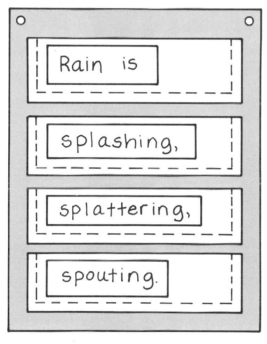

Rain is

splashing,

splattering,

spouting.

Choose a letter or letter blend:

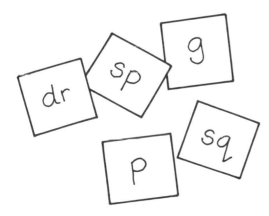

dr   sp   g   p   sq

Rain is dripping, dropping, drizzling.
Rain is pouring, puddling, pitter-pattering.

Rain Maker

dish of ice cubes

Look for raindrops on the bottom of the dish.

water in a glass pot

hot plate on low heat

Did you know?
Raindrops form when water vapor (water in the form of a gas) rises and hits cool air.

Before and After

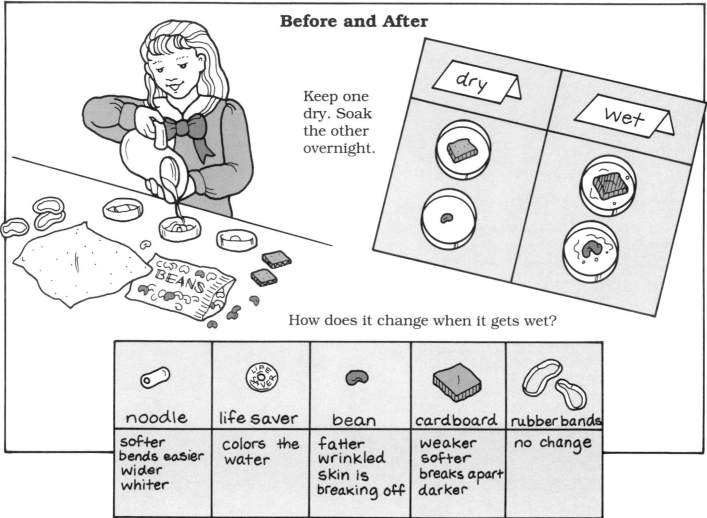

Keep one dry. Soak the other overnight.

dry

wet

How does it change when it gets wet?

noodle	life saver	bean	cardboard	rubber bands
softer bends easier wider whiter	colors the water	fatter wrinkled skin is breaking off	weaker softer breaks apart darker	no change

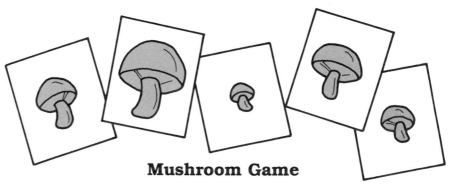

Mushroom Game

The game board and mushroom cards are on page 55.

The children play in groups with the mushroom cards placed randomly on the game board. Each player gets a turn to switch one pair of mushrooms. The object is to get all the mushrooms in order of size from biggest to smallest or from smallest to biggest.

THEMEWORKS™ : Rain
©1991 Creative Publications

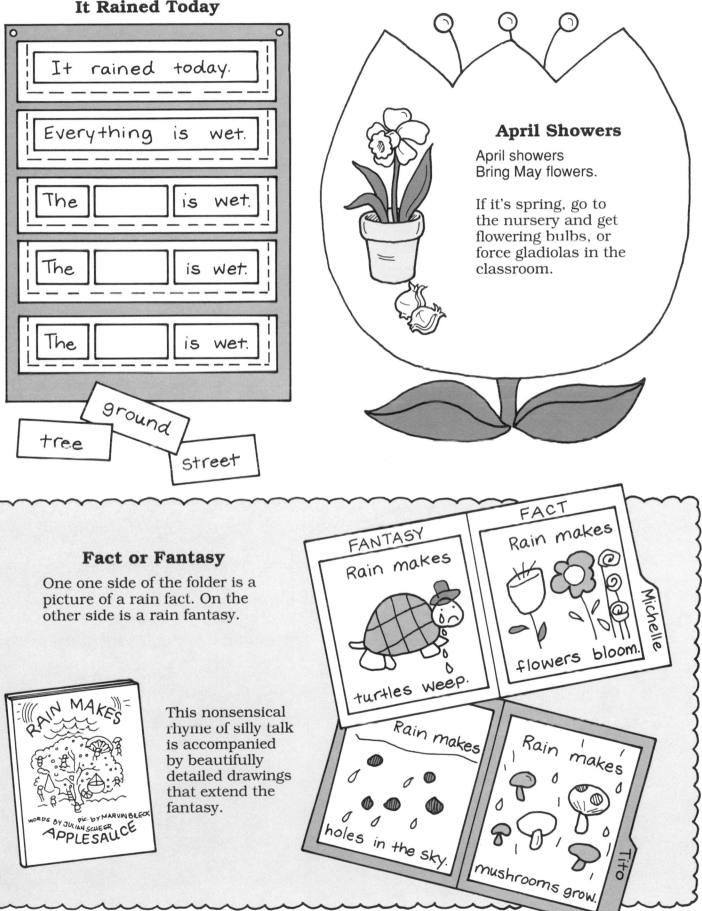

It Rained Today

It rained today.

Everything is wet.

The ___ is wet.

The ___ is wet.

The ___ is wet.

ground

tree

street

April Showers

April showers
Bring May flowers.

If it's spring, go to the nursery and get flowering bulbs, or force gladiolas in the classroom.

Fact or Fantasy

One one side of the folder is a picture of a rain fact. On the other side is a rain fantasy.

This nonsensical rhyme of silly talk is accompanied by beautifully detailed drawings that extend the fantasy.

RAIN MAKES

WORDS BY JULIAN SCHEER
PIC. BY MARVIN BILECK
APPLESAUCE

FANTASY
Rain makes
turtles weep.

FACT
Rain makes
flowers bloom.

Michelle

Rain makes
holes in the sky.

Rain makes
mushrooms grow.

Tito

Puddle Study

• Look at reflections in puddles.

• Find the deepest puddle. Measure depth with a stick.

• Find the biggest puddle. Measure the distance around (the circumference) with string.

• Draw around a puddle with chalk. Check later to see how the size of the puddle has changed.

Water Painting

Water painting is a fun way to learn about evaporation. All you need are brushes and buckets or cans of water and a playground or sidewalk. When children paint with the water, they can observe how quickly their pictures disappear depending on what kind of surface they are working on and how much sunlight their picture gets.

???????????????????????????????

Question Box

Where does the puddle water go?
The water in a puddle evaporates; that is, drops of water change to water vapor (invisible water droplets in the air). Heat in the form of sunlight quickens the evaporation process. So a puddle in the sun will dry up more quickly than a puddle in the shade.

Children can observe this process by setting out two trays, each with the same small amount of water. One can be placed in a warm, sunny part of the classroom and the other can be placed in the shade. Which dries up faster?

THEMEWORKS™ : Rain
©1991 Creative Publications

On the Bookshelf

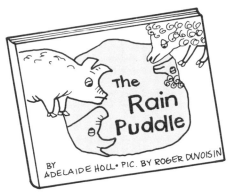

In this classic, a hen sees her reflection in a puddle and thinks another hen has fallen in. Only when the puddle evaporates do the barnyard animals stop worrying.

Studying Reflections

drawing

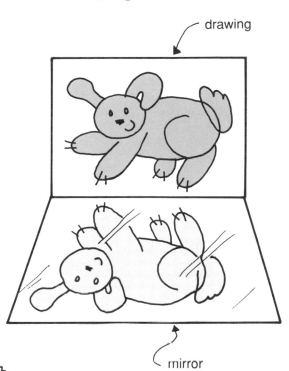

mirror

Be My Mirror

Pairs of children take turns making mirror images of each other.

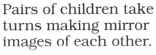

Puddle Jumping

For this game, several puddles need to be drawn with chalk on the playground. The children are to race from one end of the playground to the other without getting their feet wet in any of the puddles. They can jump over the puddles or go around them, but their feet are not to land in any of the puddles.

Contrasting Environments

We set up two environments in the classroom—a desert and a jungle—and we compare the plants and animals in these two opposite climates.

Note: The desert environment should be placed on the sunnier side of the classroom.

The children each choose a desert or jungle animal to create. Birds are hung from the ceiling while land animals are tacked to the appropriate mural or placed on the floor.

mural

THE DESERT

THE JUNGLE

Some tropical house plants: African violets, orchids, begonias, ferns, and philodendron. Venus' flytraps are especially interesting to explore.

Plant Questions to Explore

• Which plants (desert or jungle) need more water?
• Which plants grow faster?
• Which plants need more light?

THEMEWORKS™ : Rain
©1991 Creative Publications

Desert or Jungle

Animals

desert	jungle
coyote	gorilla
camel	tiger
scorpion	rhinoceros
lizard	anteater
rattlesnake	parrot
jackrabbit	toucan
vulture	sloth

How is it different?

desert	jungle
dry	rainy
sunny	shaded
sand	soil
brown	green
little life	lots of animals and plants

Classroom Pets

The children can help design a terrarium for a desert or jungle animal such as a lizard or praying mantis. Sand or soil, rocks, and plant life should be gathered and placed in the terrarium to create a desert or jungle environment similar to the one the animal inhabits in the wild. Care of the animal can be rotated among the children.

Lizzie Lizard

Places to Visit

- Zoo
- Science museum
- Arboretum or flower conservatory
- Plant shops

Reference Books

Tropical Fruit Smoothies

For each child:
⅛ cup yogurt
¼ cup milk
½ cup fresh tropical
   fruit (banana, papaya,
   mango, pineapple)

Mix in a blender until smooth.
Pour into a glass and drink.

Visit a green grocer or
produce stand to see
unusual tropical fruits.

Jungle Puppets

The children research different jungle
animals, create paper bag puppets of
the animals, and report to the class
on what they have learned about the
animal. The puppets can also be used
in dramatic play.

paper bag puppets

The Jungle Book From A to Zoo

Aa is for anteater.
Anteaters live in the jungle.

Bb is for bamboo.
Pandas eat bamboo.

Cc is for coconut.
Coconuts grow on trees.

Dd is for dark.
The jungle is shady, rainy, and dark.

Ee is for everyone.
Everyone needs the jungle.

Ff is for ferns.
There are many ferns in the jungle.

Gorillas live in the jungle.

THEMEWORKS™ : Rain
©1991 Creative Publications

Things Made of Rubber

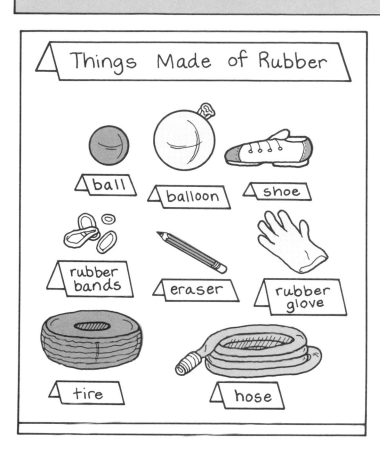

ball

balloon

shoe

rubber bands

eraser

rubber glove

tire

hose

Spice Match

Most spices come from the tropics, and their rich aromas make for this interesting sensory discrimination activity:

Cover spice containers (two of each kind) with tape so that the labels are hidden. Then open the shaker tops (with the little holes). Challenge the children to use sense of smell alone to find the pairs of containers that match.

Spices to use: black pepper, chili pepper, cinnamon, cloves, ginger, nutmeg, paprika.

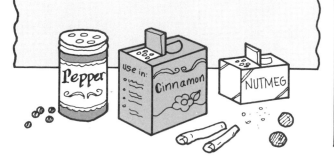

On the Bookshelf

Life in the rain forest is threatened by a machine.

In his dream, a boy visits the jungle.

A man chopping down a kapok tree learns why the tree is important to forest life.

Save the Rain Forest Posters

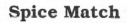

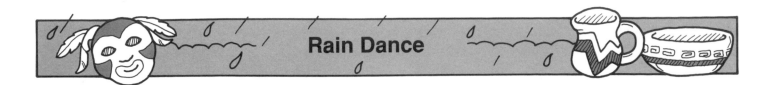

Dancing for Rain

The Hopi Indians of the American Southwest live in an arid land, where rainfall is critical for survival. Each year in August, nine days are devoted to a celebration of rain.

Gourd Rattles

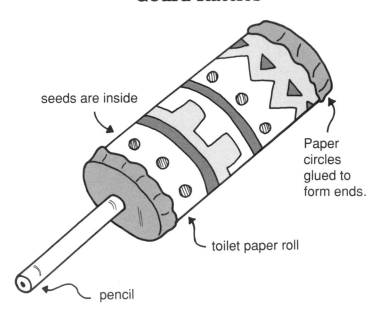

seeds are inside

Paper circles glued to form ends.

toilet paper roll

pencil

The children can experiment to find which kinds of seeds and how many seeds make the best sounds in their paper-roll gourds. Let them compare the different sounds their finished gourds make. Does the sound remind them of rain?

Baker's Dough Beads

1 cup flour
¼ cup salt
⅓ cup water

Mix flour and salt. Add water. Form the beads around a straw, then remove the straw to form an opening. The beads can be a variety of sizes and shapes. Place the shapes on foil and bake at a high temperature until the beads are hard but not brown.

After the beads are baked, they can be painted in different colors and strung in patterns.

Bead Necklaces

long, long, short, long, long, short...

Face Painting

In the traditional rain dance of the Hopi, participants blackened their faces with soot and covered their chins with white clay.

The children can get in the spirit of the ceremony by daubing white cold cream on their chins. More elaborate face painting is also possible.

Fry Bread

¼ cup white flour
¼ cup whole wheat flour
¼ teaspoon baking powder
½ teaspoon sugar
pinch of salt
¼ cup warm water

Mix, knead, and roll out the dough. Cut into squares, rectangles, triangles, diamonds, or circles.

Fry in hot oil.

Serve warm with honey.

Rain Chants

The class can create chants to sing in the ceremony.

Rain, rain
Come again.
Plants need rain.
Animals need rain.
People need rain.
Rivers need rain.
Everything needs rain.

During the rain dance, the teacher can read each line of the chant and the children can repeat it as they shake their gourd rattles.

Hopi Snake Dance

Dancers form in groups of three: One carries a snake, a second carries a feathered wand, which is used to stroke the snake, and the third is a runner. After the groups circle four times, the snakes are thrown into the center of the circle and the runners pick them up and run in different directions, setting the snakes free in the desert.

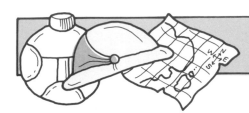

Dramatic Play: Safari

The children can journey to the desert or jungle environments in their classrooms.

Dress-Up Clothes
sun hats
kaftans
bush hats
umbrellas
khaki shorts
ponchos

Props
binoculars
ham radio
headphones
sunglasses
ice chest
water bags
map
clock
thermometer

binoculars made with two toilet paper rolls

moveable dials with brad fasteners

Safari Jeep

Making Lists

What We Will Need	
☼ desert 〰	◦◦ jungle 🍃
lots of water	raingear
food	ice chest
sunglasses	insect repellent
ice chest	

Check the Gauges

Gauges with moveable dials can be attached to the safari jeep's dashboard.

cold — temperature — hot   low — water — high

empty — fuel — full   low — speed — high

On their safaris, the children should check the gauges frequently to make sure the engine is not getting too hot, and the fuel and water levels are not getting too low.

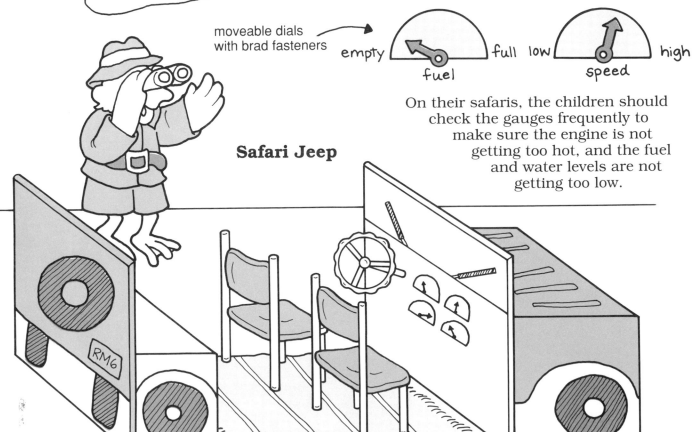

RM6

THEMEWORKS™ : Rain
©1991 Creative Publications

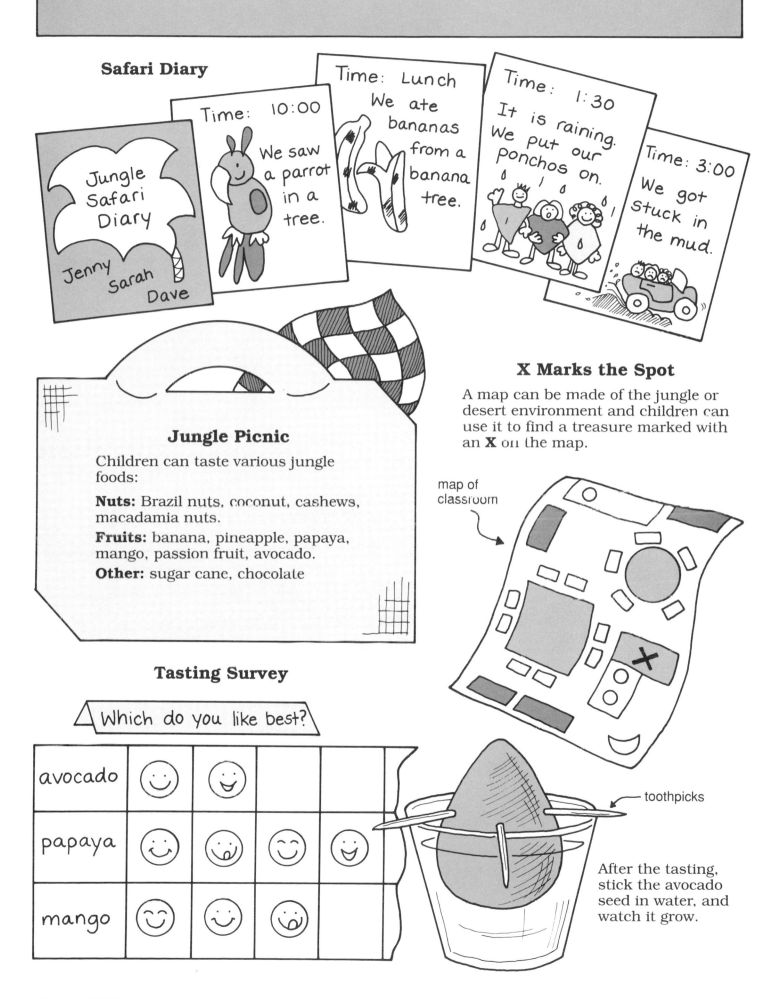

Safari Diary

Jungle Safari Diary

Jenny Sarah Dave

Time: 10:00 We saw a parrot in a tree.

Time: Lunch We ate bananas from a banana tree.

Time: 1:30 It is raining. We put our ponchos on.

Time: 3:00 We got stuck in the mud.

Jungle Picnic

Children can taste various jungle foods:

Nuts: Brazil nuts, coconut, cashews, macadamia nuts.

Fruits: banana, pineapple, papaya, mango, passion fruit, avocado.

Other: sugar cane, chocolate

X Marks the Spot

A map can be made of the jungle or desert environment and children can use it to find a treasure marked with an **X** on the map.

map of classroom

Tasting Survey

Which do you like best?

avocado	☺	☺		
papaya	☺	☺	☺	☺
mango	☺	☺	☺	

toothpicks

After the tasting, stick the avocado seed in water, and watch it grow.

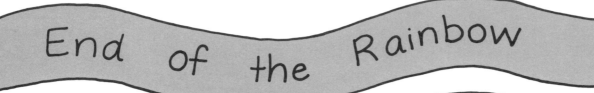

End of the Rainbow

Rainbow Parade

In the culminating event of our study of rain, we make a rainbow on the classroom floor, walk the rainbow path, drop our wishes in a pot of gold, improvise a flower dance and eat honey cakes.

Rainbow Path

Each band of the rainbow path could be a collage of objects in that color.

Rainbows have seven bands of color. From top to bottom, the colors are:

red
orange
yellow
green
blue
indigo
violet

48

THEMEWORKS™ : Rain
©1991 Creative Publications

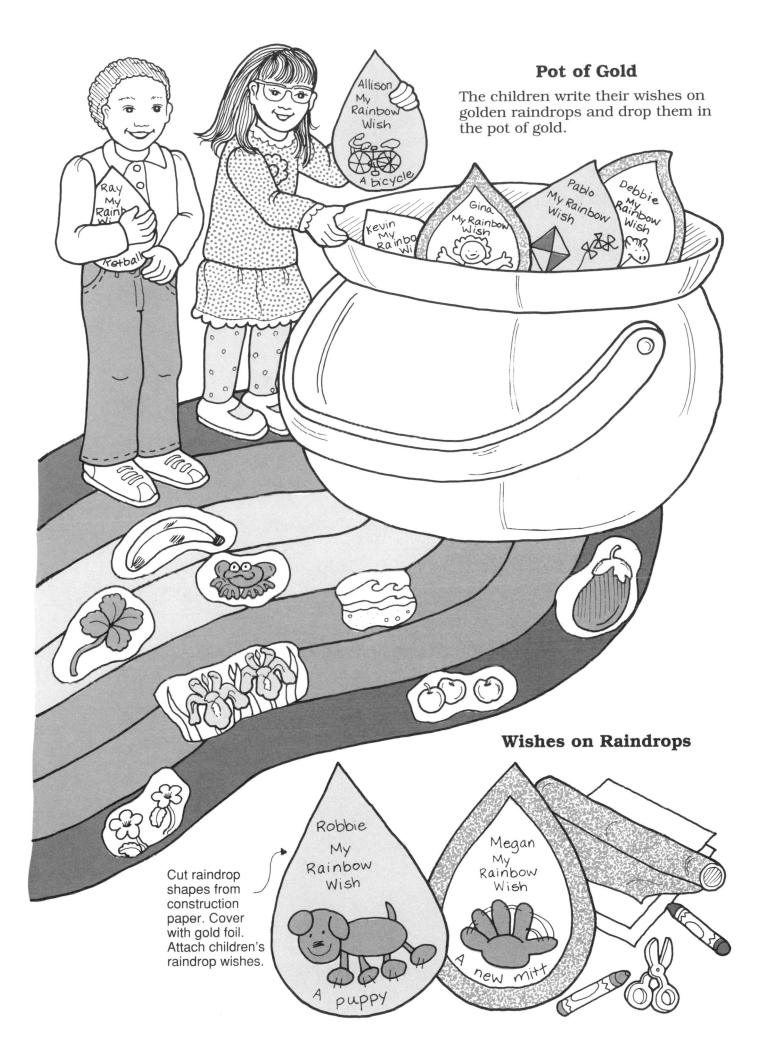

Pot of Gold

The children write their wishes on golden raindrops and drop them in the pot of gold.

Wishes on Raindrops

Cut raindrop shapes from construction paper. Cover with gold foil. Attach children's raindrop wishes.

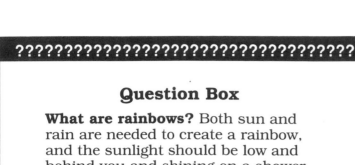
Question Box

What are rainbows? Both sun and rain are needed to create a rainbow, and the sunlight should be low and behind you and shining on a shower of rain. When the light from the sun shines on a raindrop, it is bent and the colors are separated into seven bands of color.

Since you may not be lucky enough to observe a real rainbow from your classroom window, you might wish to provide some prisms for the children to explore.

On the Bookshelf

Little Bird finds a pot of gold (honey) at the end of the rainbow and Bear makes honey cakes.

I LIKE this book.

Honey Cakes

⅓ cup honey
3 tablespoons butter
1 cup buttermilk
1 egg

1 cup flour
1 cup bran
1 teaspoon baking soda
pinch of salt

Melt honey and butter. Add buttermilk and egg. Mix dry ingredients and add honey mixture. Pour into muffin cups and bake at 350° for 30 minutes.

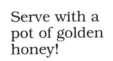

Serve with a pot of golden honey!

THEMEWORKS™ : Rain
©1991 Creative Publications

Flowers in the Rain: An Improvisation

Roles: Flowers
Clouds
Raindrops
Rainbow

Music: Melancholy music for the beginning followed by spirited dance music.

Whoever plays the rainbow can carry a streamer of rainbow colors.

Raindrops can hold popsicle® stick masks and use the gourd rattles from page 44 to make rain shower sounds.

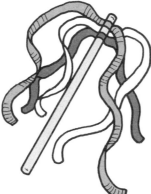

Flowers can make paper plate masks to attach to popsicle® sticks or tongue depressors.

Clouds can wear white T-shirts and headbands with cotton balls glued on. Wristbands would be fun too.

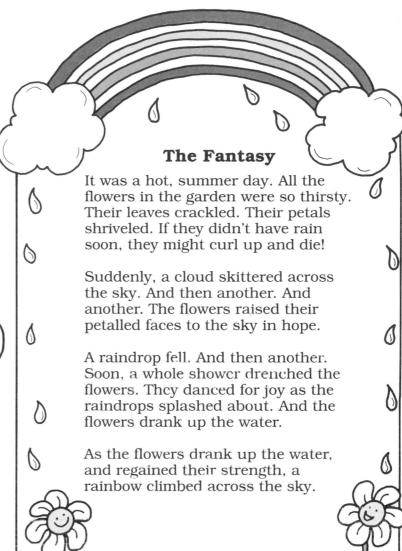

The Fantasy

It was a hot, summer day. All the flowers in the garden were so thirsty. Their leaves crackled. Their petals shriveled. If they didn't have rain soon, they might curl up and die!

Suddenly, a cloud skittered across the sky. And then another. And another. The flowers raised their petalled faces to the sky in hope.

A raindrop fell. And then another. Soon, a whole shower drenched the flowers. They danced for joy as the raindrops splashed about. And the flowers drank up the water.

As the flowers drank up the water, and regained their strength, a rainbow climbed across the sky.

Good bye! Rainbows are for all of us to share.

I'm a cloud.

Boot and Umbrella Cards

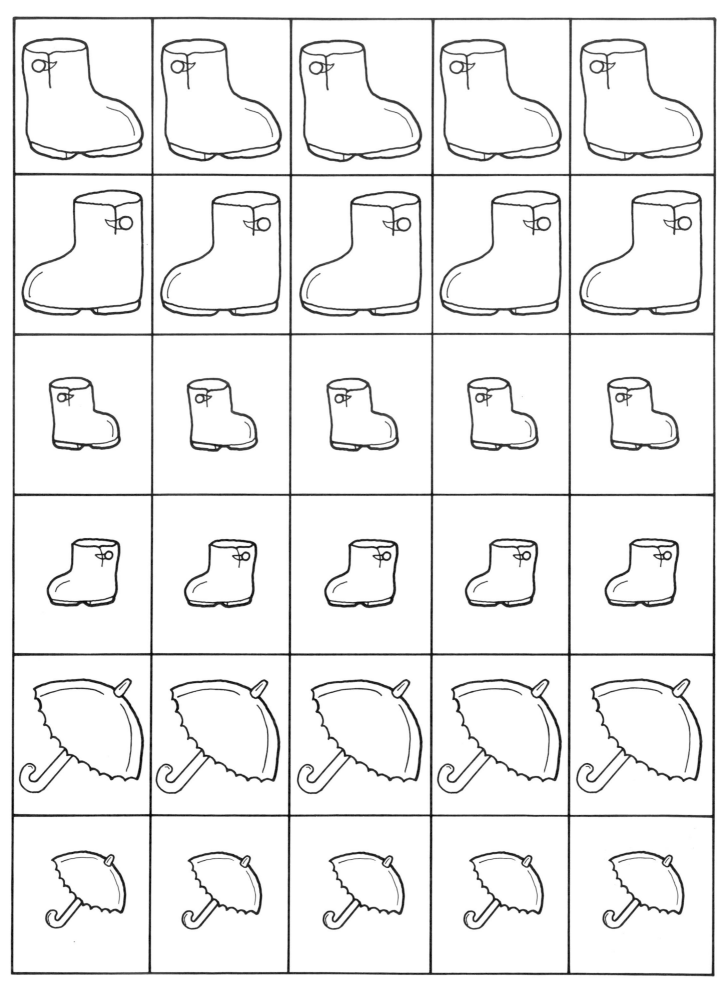

THEMEWORKS™ : Rain

Paper Doll

THEMEWORKS™ : Rain
©1991 Creative Publications

Weather Symbols

sunny	cloudy	partly cloudy
rainy	lightning	snow
hail	rainbow	foggy

Mushroom Game

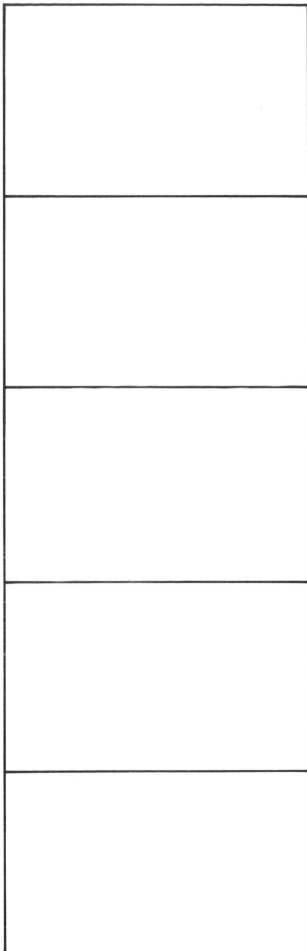

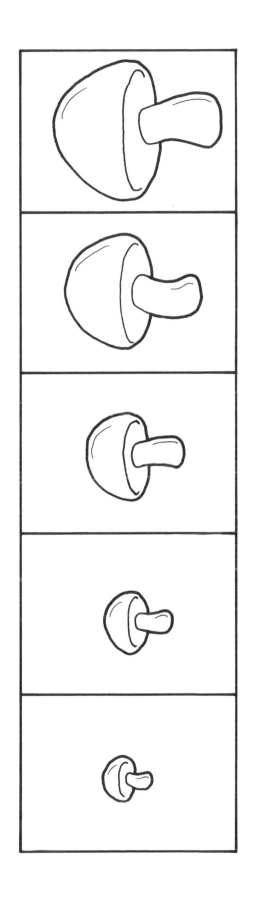

THEMEWORKS™ : Rain
©1991 Creative Publications

Picture Cards

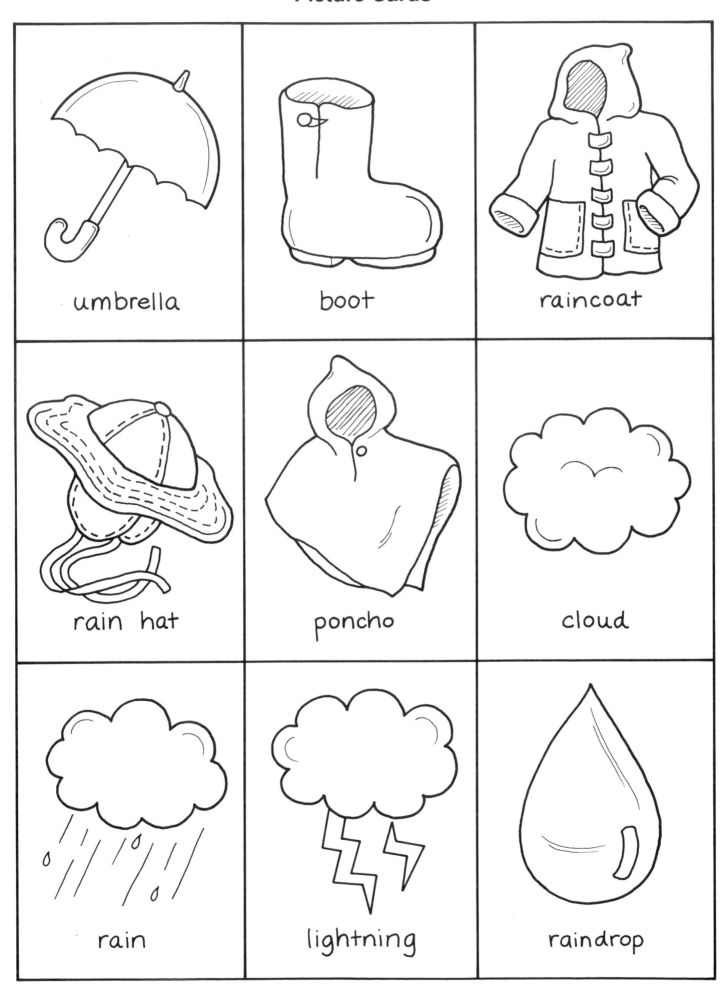

umbrella	boot	raincoat
rain hat	poncho	cloud
rain	lightning	raindrop

Picture Cards

sun

rainbow

duck

mushroom

parrot

camel

cactus

fern

banana

THEMEWORKS™ : Rain
©1991 Creative Publications

Curriculum Chart

	Language	Mathematics	Science	Social Studies	Art	Cooking	Music/Movement	P.E.	Dramatic Play
Rainwear Fashion Show pp. 10 - 11	• poem • vocabulary	• classifying • patterns		• clothing and climate			• parody		• puppet
Rainy Day Clothes pp. 12 - 13	• story • interview • poem	• measurement • classifying • money • seriation • tally count • graphing	• absorbency experiments • ducks	• occupations • clothing	• clothing design				• clothing store
Will It Rain? pp. 14 - 15	• proverbs • writing • rhymes • speaking • interview	• graphing	• weather forecasting	• folklore • occupations	• drawings • self-portraits				• weather forecaster
Cloud Watching pp. 16 - 17	• experience chart • story	• temperature • size/shape • time	• clouds	• timeline	• photography • collage			• creative movement	
Cloud Play pp. 18 - 19	• story • language frame • similes	• measurement	• trans-formations		• mobile	• cloud pudding	• parody	• tag	

THEMEWORKS™ : Rain
©1991 Creative Publications

Curriculum Chart

	Language	Mathematics	Science	Social Studies	Art	Cooking	Music/Movement	P.E.	Dramatic Play
A Chance of Rain pp. 20 - 21	• vocabulary • story • writing	• measurement • estimation • counting	• cloud types • cloud demo	• African folktale	• fingerpaint • drawing	• cloud paint			
It's Raining It's Pouring pp. 22 - 23	• diary • vocabulary	• time • graphing	• rain types • predictions		• drawing		• song	• creative movement	• role playing
Rain, Rain Everywhere pp. 24 - 25	• rhyme frame • story • poem • idiom • writing	• measurement • estimation • conservation of volume	• terrarium • rain levels		• drawing • printing				
A Walk in the Rain pp. 26 - 27	• captions • stories • new verses	• time • measurement	• drainage • animals in the rain		• photography		• song		
The Rain Walk Continues pp. 28 - 29	• poem • describing • language frame	• measurement • time	• five senses			• soup	• percussion instruments	• creative movement	

Curriculum Chart

	Language	Mathematics	Science	Social Studies	Art	Cooking	Music/Movement	P.E.	Dramatic Play
It Rained and It Rained pp. 30 - 31	• story • storybook comparisons	• shapes • number • counting • graphing	• animals • sink or float	• traditional story	• clay figures • construction • shape collage		• song		• story acting
Rainy Day Blues pp. 32 - 33	• language frame • poetry • story	• calendar • counting • measurement	• weather • animal movement	• feelings	• peek-a-book	• peanut butter fudge	• song	• creative movement	
Raindrops Keep Falling pp. 34 - 35	• poems • alliteration • story	• number song	• raindrop observations • rain demo		• blow painting		• parody		
Changes, Changes, Changes pp. 36 - 37	• experience chart • story • language frames • rhyme • poem • writing	• seriation	• changes from soaking • bulb planting • cause and effect	• fact vs. fantasy	• drawing				
Rain Puddles pp. 38 - 39	• story	• measurement • time	• reflections • evaporation		• painting • drawing			• mirror reflections • foot race	

60

Curriculum Chart

	Language	Mathematics	Science	Social Studies	Art	Cooking	Music/Movement	P.E.	Dramatic Play
Desert and Jungle pp. 40 - 41	• opposites		• plants • animals • plant care • animal care	• habitats • deserts • jungles	• mural • construction				
Jungle Potpourri pp. 42 - 43	• oral reports • phonics • captions • slogans • stories	• measurement	• jungle animals • fruits • sensory discrimination	• occupations • rubber products • rain forest ecology	• puppets • posters • A-B-C book	• fruit smoothie			• puppetry
Rain Dance pp. 44 - 45	• chants	• measurement • size/shape • patterns • geometric shapes	• sounds	• Indian rain ceremonies • desert life	• bead necklaces • face painting • rattles	• baker's dough • fry bread	• gourd rattles	• rain dance	
Bold Journeys pp. 46 - 47	• lists • diary	• measurement terms • time • survey	• seed	• needs/wants • jungle foods • map reading	• construction	• tasting party			• safari
End of the Rainbow pp. 48 - 51	• writing • story	• measurement • time	• rainbows	• wishes	• collage • streamer	• honey cakes	• musical accompaniment	• creative movement	

THEMEWORKS™ : Rain
©1991 Creative Publications

Resource List

Stories

Asch, Frank. *SkyFire*. New York: Prentice-Hall, 1984.

Carrick, Carol. *Lost in the Storm*. Seabury Press, 1974.

Cherry, Lynne. *The Great Kapok Tree: A Tale of the Amazon Rain Forest*. Orlando: Harcourt Brace, 1990.

Cowcher, Helen. *Rain Forest*. New York: Farrar, Straus and Giroux, 1988.

Ginsburg, Mirra. *Mushroom in the Rain*. New York: Macmillan, 1974.

Holl, Adelaide. *The Rain Puddle*. New York: Lothrop, Lee, and Shepard, 1965.

Keller, Holly. *Will It Rain?* New York: Greenwillow, 1984.

Rayner, Mary. *The Rain Cloud*. New York: Atheneum, 1980.

Ryder, Joanne. *A Wet and Sandy Day*. New York: Harper and Row, 1977.

Scheffler, Ursel. *A Walk in the Rain*. New York: Putnam, 1986.

Shaw, Charles G. *It Looked Like Spilt Milk*. New York: Harper & Row, 1947.

Shulevitz, Uri. *Rain Rain Rivers*. New York: Farrar, Straus and Giroux, 1969.

Soya, Kiyosha. *A House of Leaves*. New York: Putnam, 1987.

Spier, Peter. *Peter Spier's Rain*. New York: Doubleday, 1982.

Stevenson, James. *We Hate Rain!* New York: Greenwillow, 1988.

Tafuri, Nancy. *Junglewalk*. New York: Greenwillow, 1988.

Tresselt, Alvin. *Rain Drop Splash*. New York: Lothrop, Lee and Shepard, 1946.

Yashima, Taro. *Umbrella*. New York: Puffin Books, 1958.

Zolotow, Charlotte. *The Storm Book*. New York: Harper & Row, 1952.

THEMEWORKS™ : Rain
©1991 Creative Publications

Fairy Tales, Folktales, Legends, and Biblical Stories

Aardeema, Verna. *Bringing the Rain to Kapiti Plain.* New York: E.P. Dutton, 1981.

Bolliger, Max. *Noah and the Rainbow: An Ancient Story.* New York: Thomas Y. Crowell, 1972.

Hogrogian, Nonny. *Noah's Ark.* New York: Knopf, 1986.

Singer, Isaac Bashevis. *Why Noah Chose the Dove.* New York: Farrar, Straus and Giroux., 1974.

Spier, Peter. *Noah's Ark.* New York: Doubleday, 1977.

Wynants, Miche. *Noah's Ark.* Orlando: Harcourt, Brace, Jovanovich, 1965.

Information

Bash, Barbara. *Desert Giant: The World of the Saguaro Cactus.* Boston: Little, Brown, 1989.

Branley, Franklyn. *Rain and Hail.* New York: Thomas Y. Crowell, 1983.

Busch, Phyllis S. *Cactus in the Desert.* New York: Thomas Y. Crowell, 1979.

Catchpole, Dr. Clive. *The Living World Deserts.* New York: E. P. Dutton, 1983.

_____. *The Living World Jungles.* New York: E. P. Dutton, 1983.

DePaola, Tomie. *The Cloud Book.* New York: Holiday House, 1975.

Goldin, Augusta. *Ducks Don't Get Wet.* New York: Thomas Y. Crowell, 1989.

Pope, Joyce. *A Closer Look at Jungles.* Gloucester Press, 1978.

Books of Poetry, Proverbs, Songs, and Rhymes

Davis, Hubert. *A January Fog Will Freeze a Hog.* Iowa City: Crown, 1977.

Emberley, Barbara. *One Wide River To Cross.* New York: Prentice-Hall, 1967.

Martin, Bill Jr. and John Archambault. *Listen to the Rain.* New York: Henry Holt, 1988.

Prelutsky, Jack. *Rainy, Rainy Saturday.* New York: Greenwillow, 1980.

Scheer, Julian. *Rain Makes Applesauce.* New York: Holiday House, 1964.

Acknowledgements

Grateful acknowledgement is made to the following for permission to reprint their copyrighted material. Every reasonable effort has been made to trace the ownership of all copyrighted material included in this book. Any errors which may have occurred are inadvertent and will be corrected in subsequent editions, provided notification is sent to the publisher.

Marchette Chute "Showers" from RHYMES ABOUT US by Marchette Chute. Copyright © 1974 by Marchette Chute. Permission to reprint granted by Mary Chute Smith.

Aileen Fisher "Raindrops" from OUT IN THE DARK AND THE DAYLIGHT by Aileen Fisher. Copyright © 1980. Reprinted by permission of Harper Collins Publishers.

A. A. Milne "Happiness" from WHEN WE WERE VERY YOUNG by A.A. MILNE. Copyright © 1924 by E.P. Dutton, renewed 1952 by A.A. Milne. Used by permission of Dutton Children's Books, a division of Penguin Books USA Inc.

William Wise "Rainy Day" from ALL ON A SUMMER DAY. Copyright © 1971 by William Wise. Reprinted by permission of William Wise.